The Fault in Our Stars:
A Reader's Guide to the John Green Novel

ROBERT CRAYOLA

CONTENTS

INTRODUCTION

Since its publication in 2012, *The Fault in Our Stars* has become John Green's bestselling work. It has gained both popular and critical acclaim, and with the release of the film adaptation in 2014 the book has risen to new levels of renown.

This guide is designed to help you navigate this remarkable novel. I will put the story in context, clarify difficult terms and passages, and give you easy access to the story. All important plot details will be revealed in this guide, so if you don't want spoilers, read the book first and then use this guide for deeper understanding.

Before we look at the novel itself, let's take a quick look at the life of its author, John Green.

AUTHOR: John Michael Green was born on August 24, 1977 in Indianapolis, Indiana, the main setting of *The Fault in Our Stars*. He and his family moved to Florida shortly after his birth, and he attended school there and in Alabama. He had a strong interest in religious studies and planned to become an Episcopal priest. While working in a hospital with children, however, he decided to become an author. He focused on young adult (YA) novels, but first he published book reviews in magazines and elsewhere.

His first novel, *Looking for Alaska*, was published in 2005, and it earned him popular and critical acclaim, and the movie rights were optioned (although no film has been made). Since that first novel, Green has authored or co-authored five additional books. *The Fault in Our Stars* has proven most popular, with over a million copies sold in its first year.

In addition to his writings, Green is also known for the popular Vlogbrothers YouTube channel that he and his brother Hank regularly update. Begun in 2007, the channel has over a million subscribers. The brothers also founded VidCon, the popular online video convention that meets each year in southern California.

Green lives in the city of his birth, Indianapolis, with his wife, two children, and their dog.

THE ELEMENTS OF LITERATURE

STRUCTURE: *The Fault in Our Stars* is divided into 25 chapters, which can be roughly divided into three sections (Hazel and Augustus falling in love, going to Amsterdam, and Augustus's death).

SETTING: The story takes place in Indianapolis, Indiana, and in Amsterdam, The Netherlands. The era is approximately the time of the book's publication (2012).

NARRATOR & P.O.V.: The book is narrated by Hazel Lancaster, a 16-year-old girl. She offers an intelligent and cynical perspective in the story.

TENSE: The book is written in the past tense.

TONE: Tone is how a book "feels." Because much of the subject matter revolves around death and cancer, the book often has a sad tone. However, Hazel has a sharp wit, and this keeps the tone from becoming melodramatic or monotonous.

PLOT: The plot is the book's story. Here is a quick snapshot of the plot. We'll take a much deeper look in the chapter summaries.

Hazel Lancaster, a teenage girl in Indiana, has cancer.

While attending a cancer support group meeting, she meets Augustus Waters and they soon fall in love. She introduces him to her favorite book, *An Imperial Affliction*, and he is able to arrange a trip to Amsterdam to meet the book's author, Peter Van Houten. When they meet him, however, Van Houten is a huge disappointment to the teens. They return to the U.S. jaded by the experience, but more in love than ever. Unfortunately, Augustus's cancer has returned and he grows increasingly ill. Hazel enjoys some final days with Augustus, but he soon dies. Hazel tries to carry on. Peter Van Houten makes a surprise appearance at Augustus's funeral. Hazel pursues Augustus's final letter and finally tracks it down. She resolves some issues with her family, and Hazel is able to make peace with herself.

That is an extremely shortened version of the story, but it gives you a general idea of where it is going. We'll look at a more detailed version of the plot soon.

PROTAGONIST: The protagonist is the main character or characters that we most sympathize with. Hazel and her boyfriend Augustus are the protagonists in the story.

ANTAGONIST: The antagonist opposes the protagonists. The main antagonist in the story isn't a person; it's the cancer that is destroying the lives of these young people.

CONFLICT: Conflict is the struggle faced by the characters. Hazel and Augustus struggle with their illnesses, but they also struggle for deeper meaning as they search for the author Peter Van Houten. Further conflict comes from the emotional upsets among their friends and families as cancer takes its toll on their lives.

CLIMAX: The climax is the moment of greatest tension in the story. Initially, it seems that the meeting with Van Houten is the climax. Once Augustus's condition is revealed, however, we realize that the true battle has only begun. The best choice for the climax is when Augustus and Hazel struggle at the gas station and it seems that he might die right there.

RESOLUTION: The resolution is how the story concludes after the climax has passed. Hazel grieves when Augustus's death finally comes. She pursues his final letter (mailed to Peter Van Houten) and gains some peace when she reads the kind things that Augustus wrote about her.

THEMES: Themes are what the author chooses to illustrate through the narrative. Some of the themes in the novel include:

Sacrifice – Hazel, her mother, Augustus, and many other characters make sacrifices to help others.

The Pain and Suffering of Life – Because many of the characters have cancer, they face physical pain and suffering. In addition to this, it might be argued that the emotional anguish characters experience is even worse.

Idealization and Expectation – Isaac expects Monica to be with him forever. Hazel expects to die before Augustus. Both Hazel and Augustus expect their meeting with Van Houten to be enjoyable and meaningful. Characters are constantly expecting things to be one way, and they suffer when things go differently. In this, they learn to accept whatever comes to them.

Fear of Dying – Fear not only of dying, but what comes after we die, is a recurring theme in the novel.

TITLE: The title for *The Fault in Our Stars* comes from the William Shakespeare play *Julius Caesar*, in which Cassius says, "The fault, dear Brutus, is not in our stars, / But in ourselves that we are underlings." Cassius rejects the popular concept of astrology, saying that we all have more power to affect our lives than anything outside of us. This can be connected to the idea that we are responsible for our own happiness, as some of the characters start to learn in the novel.

More literally, the cancer itself can be viewed as a "fault" in ourselves.

CHARACTERS

HAZEL GRACE LANCASTER – Hazel is a sixteen-year-old girl and the narrator of the book. She has cancer that has affected her thyroid gland, and more recently, her lungs. She must have a machine with her to breathe. She is intelligent, sarcastic, and largely isolated by her illness. She does attend community college and occasionally goes to a cancer support group, where she meets Augustus Waters, whom she rapidly falls in love with. Her favorite book is *An Imperial Affliction*.

AUGUSTUS WATERS – Augustus is a boy Hazel meets at her cancer support group. He is handsome, kind, funny, and generally more optimistic than Hazel. His own battle with cancer forced him to have one of his legs amputated. He initially sees Hazel as a ghostly reminder of his dead ex-girlfriend, but he soon learns to love Hazel on her own merits. His cancer will come back and kill him by the end of the book.

ISAAC – Isaac is a friend of both Hazel and Augustus. He is deeply in love with his girlfriend Monica at the beginning of the book, but she leaves him when he is forced to have an eye operation, leaving him blind. Isaac has a dark wit, especially once he loses his sight, but he also has perseverance.

HAZEL'S MOM (Mrs. Lancaster) – Hazel's mom is her closest friend, and Hazel thinks her mom will be devastated by her death from cancer. Mrs. Lancaster has devoted her life to her daughter, and she reveals near the end of the book that she's been studying (in secret) to be a social worker.

HAZEL'S DAD (Mr. Lancaster) – Hazel's dad is loving and supportive of his daughter, although not as familiar with the details the way Hazel's mother is.

PATRICK – A cancer survivor himself, Patrick leads the support group that Hazel, Isaac, and Augustus attend. He has lost his testicles to testicular cancer, which Hazel often references humorously. He facilitates the support group with optimism, humor, and warmth.

PETER VAN HOUTEN – Van Houten is the author of Hazel's favorite book, *An Imperial Affliction*. She has many questions about the book and goes to Amsterdam with Augustus to meet the author. What she finds there is disappointing: a drunk old man who is cynical, angry, and antisocial. Later, he'll fly to America to attend Augustus's funeral, and resolve some things with Hazel.

LIDEWIJ VLIEGENTHART – The personal assistant to Peter Van Houten. Lidewij arranged the meeting between Van Houten, Hazel, and Augustus. She is patient and kind, the opposite of Van Houten. Lidewij resigns when Van Houten is exceptionally rude to Hazel and Augustus.

KAITLYN – One of Hazel's few remaining friends from her public school days. Kaitlyn is slightly pretentious, but cares about Hazel and her illness. Hazel likes her, yet she can't totally relate to Kaitlyn (because of her illness) and sometimes needs to get away from her.

AUGUSTUS'S PARENTS – Almost excessively optimistic and upbeat, Augustus's parents are supportive of their son but sometimes question his decisions as his cancer recurs. Hazel thinks they view their son differently than she does.

CAROLINE MATHERS – Augustus's dead ex-girlfriend. Augustus met her at the hospital when she had brain cancer. Her illness negatively affected her personality, and Augustus had to deal with her moodiness and cruelty until she died.

DR. MARIA – Hazel's primary doctor for handling her cancer treatment. Dr. Maria goes beyond her role as a doctor to truly care about Hazel, arguing for her trip to Amsterdam with Augustus.

CHAPTER SUMMARIES & COMMENTARY

CHAPTER 1: The book's narrator, Hazel Lancaster, begins by telling us that she is sixteen, and that she has cancer. Immediately we see that Hazel is humorous, but it is a dark humor because of her ever-present cancer, and she uses a great deal of sarcasm.

Her mother thinks Hazel is depressed and has made her join a support group that meets in the basement of a local church. The group is led by a cancer survivor named Patrick. Although Hazel is cynical of the group and critical of many things about the group, she seems to receive some benefit from the social contact, although she will never admit it. Out of high school for the past three years, Hazel is largely isolated (although we'll later learn she attends community college), and describes her parents as her two best friends.

The support group is for teenagers with cancer. Hazel originally had thyroid cancer, which has spread to a "satellite colony in [her] lungs." She must take a breathing machine with her everywhere just to stay alive.

A boy named Isaac is the best thing about her support

group. He has cancer of the eye and his sarcasm and cynicism are a match for Hazel's. He has brought a friend with him to the group, a tall boy named Augustus Waters. Augustus seems to have made a recovery from his cancer and is mainly there to support Isaac, who will have an operation on his eyes in a few weeks that will leave him blind.

Augustus and Hazel are immediately attracted to each other. Hazel makes a comment on something Augustus says about oblivion, paraphrasing a section of her favorite book. She basically says that since all humanity will eventually die and be forgotten, you don't need to worry about your death and oblivion. This book that she refers to is *An Imperial Affliction*, written by Peter Van Houten, who will play a key role in the book. But for now, just know that it is Hazel's favorite book and she has read it many times.

Augustus invites Hazel to his home to watch *V for Vendetta* (he says she looks like Natalie Portman in the movie). She notices a limp in Augustus's walk and guesses (correctly) that he has a prosthetic leg. Hazel considers going with Augustus, but then he puts a cigarette in his mouth. This is a major deal breaker for her. She can't understand how someone who has had cancer could give money to a corporation to give Augustus even more cancer. She finds herself suddenly disgusted with Augustus. But he tells her that he *doesn't* actually smoke. He only puts an unlit cigarette in his mouth for reassurance. He says, "You put the killing thing right between your teeth, but you don't give it the power to do its killing."

Not entirely convinced, Hazel is willing to give Augustus a chance. She tells her mom about the plan to see *V for Vendetta* and leaves with Augustus.

CHAPTER 2: Augustus is a bad driver, jerkily braking and revving up – he has poor control of the pedals with his prosthetic leg.

At this time, Hazel tells us more about her medical history, about how she was taken out of school and had some painful treatments and surgery, finally getting some relief from her tumors with the help of an experimental drug.

She tries to paint a more optimistic picture of herself for Augustus, and tells him she earned a high school diploma (a GED) and now takes community college classes.

At Augustus's house, Hazel finds that sentences are engraved or sewn all over the place, cheerfully optimistic (or *painfully* optimistic to Hazel) messages reminding people to cheer up. Augustus's family calls them *encouragements*. Hazel meets his parents and finds them nice, although she's far more cynical than they are.

Augustus wants to watch *V for Vendetta* in the basement (perhaps to put the moves on Hazel), but his father insists they watch it in the living room. As this takes place, Hazel tries to determine her feelings for Augustus, and seems to have settled on a healthy infatuation for him.

Before the movie, Augustus shows Hazel his basketball trophies in the basement. He enjoyed basketball for a while until he realized how futile it all was. He remembers the day before his operation, and the realization his sporting life would never be the same again.

He turns to Hazel and tries to discover her hobbies. She's a little reserved, but finally tells Augustus about her favorite book, *An Imperial Affliction*. He immediately plans to read it. He gives her a copy of *The Price of Dawn*, a shallow novelization of Augustus's favorite video game. Although it doesn't look like a very profound read, the book symbolizes a bond between the new friends.

She drives home with Augustus. It seems like they might kiss, and he asks to see her again tomorrow. She tries to take it slowly, but knows that she wants to see him soon. She says she'll call him when she finishes reading *The Price of Dawn*.

CHAPTER 3: Hazel stays up late reading the novel Augustus gave her. It's a bit below her usual reading standards, but she enjoys it because it came from *him*. The next morning, her mother has to wake her so she isn't later for her literature class at the college. Her mom also wishes her a happy "thirty-third half birthday" (making Hazel sixteen-and-a-half). Her parents' enthusiasm is sometimes at odds with Hazel's own low-key cynicism.

Hazel makes plans with her friend Kaitlyn to meet at the mall that afternoon. Although she agrees to this, she says she wants to be alone sometimes, and that she can't really connect to people who haven't had an experience similar to her own. She waits for Kaitlyn at the mall and reads further into the adventures of Max Mayhem (the hero of the novel series Augustus recommended). She appreciates that Mayhem's adventures "kept happening." She then shops with Kaitlyn a while, but Hazel says she has to leave soon and parts with her friend. In reality, she just wants some more alone time.

She reads, and then a little girl uninhibitedly asks about Hazel's breathing device. Hazel lets the girl try it herself. She appreciates that the girl isn't self-conscious and doesn't treat Hazel like she is "different."

CHAPTER 4: Hazel begins this chapter with a

summary of the book she has mentioned a few times, *An Imperial Affliction* (*AIA*). It's her favorite book. It concerns a girl named Anna who gets cancer, but it's not a "cancer book," as Hazel puts it, meaning that it doesn't have the usual clichés and sentimentality associated with narratives about the dying. There is also a lot about the book's characters, particularly Anna's mother and the "Dutch Tulip Man," who may or may not be a sinister figure. The book ends with an unfinished sentence, which indicates to Hazel that Anna has died. The lack of closure frustrated Hazel and she's written several letters to the author (Peter Van Houten) asking what happened to the characters. She has received no response.

Hazel gets in touch with Augustus to tell him about reading *The Price of Dawn*. Augustus is still reading *AIA*, but he's already 453 pages into it. She says they can meet again when he's done. He immediately hangs up the phone to continue his reading.

The next day he texts her and is similarly frustrated by *AIA*'s inconclusive ending. She phones him to discuss it. Instead, she learns Isaac is at Augustus's house and in bad shape. She agrees to come over right away. She drives there and finds Augustus and Isaac playing video games. Isaac is crying because his girlfriend Monica dumped him. She didn't want the heartache of being with a blind person after his eye operation. They play more video games and destroy Augustus's basketball trophies with a cathartic rage. It's not about whether it makes Isaac feel "better" or not. As Augustus says (quoting *AIA*), "That's the thing about pain. It demands to be felt."

CHAPTER 5: A week passes and Augustus hasn't called Hazel. Then during dinner one day his call finally comes. They discuss *AIA* and how the book's author,

Peter Van Houten, hasn't written anything since that book. To Hazel's surprise and delight, Augustus reveals that he has gotten in touch with Van Houten's assistant, through which he has communicated with Van Houten himself. The tone in Van Houten's message is largely pessimistic, though he does thank Augustus for enjoying his book.

Hazel gets the email of Van Houten's assistant, a woman named Lidewij Vliegenthart, and sends her own message to Van Houten. She is intensely curious about what happens to the characters in *AIA*.

Hazel and Augustus begin to discuss each other. She confides that she hasn't kissed anyone in years. As for Augustus, he hasn't kissed anyone since his ex-girlfriend Caroline nearly a year ago. Hazel asks further questions and learns that Caroline is dead.

A few days pass and Van Houten's assistant hasn't replied to Hazel's email. Isaac's eye surgery has taken place. He is now blind, but at least the cancer seems to be gone. Hazel visits him at the hospital and it's obvious he's still sad about the breakup with his girlfriend Monica.

A message finally arrives from Van Houten. He says he doesn't want to reveal any further details about his characters through email or over the phone, but that he'd be willing to discuss it further in person. This astonishes Hazel and she tells her mom, who reminds Hazel of the expense involved in traveling to Amsterdam. She also tells Augustus. He asks about her wish through the Genie Foundation (similar to a real organization, the Make-a-Wish Foundation, that grants "wishes" to children with life-threatening medical conditions), but Hazel admits she used it when she was thirteen to visit Disney World. In the course of their conversation Augustus casually mentions that he has a crush on Hazel. This thrills her, but she keeps it to herself.

A few days later Augustus brings flowers to Hazel and meets her parents. They like him. He takes Hazel with him to a surprise location. It's an outdoor sculpture park that Hazel has never been to. They eat sandwiches and Augustus has included Dutch symbols everywhere he can (in the food, his clothes, and the location). He then reveals the big surprise: He still has *his* wish from the Genie Foundation, and he wants to use it to take Hazel with him to Amsterdam, from May 3-7.

CHAPTER 6: Hazel tells her mom about Augustus's plan to use his wish to take her to Amsterdam. Her mom is pleased, but concerned. They talk to Hazel's physician, Dr. Maria, who wants someone knowledgeable about Hazel's condition along on the trip – hence Hazel's mom will be going with them on the trip as well.

Hazel is anxious about "prostituting" her friendship with Augustus to finance the trip. She talks with her friend Kaitlyn about a new boy she's met (without mentioning Augustus by name). Kaitlyn deduces that it *is* Augustus and confirms with Hazel that he is attractive. So why is Hazel acting all weird? Kaitlyn suggests Hazel is practicing *preemptive dumping*, avoiding future problems with Augustus by stopping the relationship before it really begins.

Hazel herself isn't exactly sure what's wrong. She searches for information about Augustus's ex-girlfriend, Caroline Mathers, and finds her profile online. Hazel notices an unsettling resemblance between herself and Caroline. She also finds a huge number of messages posted for the dead girl. One of these messages particularly haunts Hazel, suggesting that Caroline's illness has wounded all those around her.

Hazel's parents notice a change in her mood and try to learn what's wrong. She asks for some alone time. She feels like a "grenade" just waiting to go off and hurt her loved ones. This connects to a major theme in the book – namely, that to love is to open yourself up to being hurt. Trying to avoid pain in others, she texts Augustus and says she can't kiss him because of the future pain it will inevitably cause. He jokes and flirts back in response, but she stays serious.

As Hazel prepares for bed, her parents assure her she is not a grenade, and that she has brought them far more joy than pain. She sleeps with her childhood toy, a stuffed bear named Bluie, for reassurance, but wakes up with a horrible pain in her head. This has an eerie correspondence to the brain cancer that killed Caroline Mathers.

CHAPTER 7: Hazel screams from the pain in her head and her parents wake and rush her to the hospital. The pain is so bad that Hazel is ready to wish she were dead. It was due to insufficient oxygen to the brain, caused by fluid that had accumulated in her lungs.

Hazel is kept at the hospital for about a week. The first few days she is largely unconscious. A kind nurse named Allison informs her that Augustus has been waiting for her patiently in the waiting room. Dr. Maria finally approves Hazel to check out of the hospital, and she sees Augustus. They discuss the trip to Amsterdam, seemingly delayed by Hazel's health troubles. Then Augustus presents a handwritten note from Peter Van Houten. Hazel reads it in awe. It's full of literary digressions and philosophizing, and Hazel loves it. She is more determined than ever to go to Amsterdam, but it will be difficult to convince her parents and doctors.

CHAPTER 8: Hazel, her parents, and doctors at the hospital have a "cancer team meeting" to discuss Hazel's health status. They decide to keep her on the experimental drug Phalanxifor, but she is in unknown territory with the treatment and nobody knows what will happen at this point. They will also continue with regular draining of the fluid in her lungs. As for visiting Amsterdam – that is questionable. She tells this to Augustus and he says he's going to die a virgin, surprising Hazel. She watches TV with her family and falls into a deep sleep.

She wakes later and is sad to see a swing set in her backyard from her childhood. She tells Augustus and he comes over to see it (but in reality wants to cheer Hazel up). They decide to give the swings away through an online ad. Then Augustus reads part of *An Imperial Affliction* to her. She still tries to keep him at a distance, but she's not trying so hard – he told her it'd be futile anyway. He sneaks a kiss and leaves. The swing set also disappears before long as well.

When Hazel checks her email she discovers that Lidewij Vliegenthart, Peter Van Houten's assistant, eagerly anticipates their arrival in Amsterdam. Hazel tells her mom to contact the Genie people and let them know the trip isn't happening, but Hazel's mom reveals a secret: The trip *will* happen. The doctors decided to allow it. Hazel is overjoyed.

CHAPTER 9: For the first time since she met Augustus, Hazel goes to her cancer support group. Isaac is also there, wearing sunglasses and led in by his mother. It's a typical meeting and Hazel tolerates it without really enjoying it.

Afterward, Isaac invites Hazel to his house. They go there and play a "video" game that doesn't use any video.

It's just a voice that talks to them and describes their situation in a fantasy world. They tell the game what they want their characters to do. As they play, they talk about Augustus. Hazel has mixed feelings about starting a relationship with Augustus. She doesn't want to hurt him as she suffers through her illness. They talk about "fault," connecting to the theme of the title. Illness may not be something that Isaac or Hazel chose, but it is a part of them, and it affects everyone they know.

CHAPTER 10: Because Hazel can't carry a suitcase, she must share one with her mom when they go to Amsterdam. They both must pack tightly. They get an early start on the day of their flight. When they arrive at Augustus's house to pick him up, they hear yelling from within. Augustus is arguing with his parents about going to Amsterdam and spending time with Hazel (it seems). Hazel texts him from the car and he comes from the house like nothing has occurred.

At the airport they go through security and Hazel removes her breathing equipment to go through the metal detector. Without oxygen she quickly struggles. It is a harsh reminder of her situation. Her mom notices and is concerned, as usual.

Before they board the plane Augustus goes to get breakfast. He takes a long time. Later, he explains to Hazel that he didn't want to see others staring at her – it makes him too angry, and he wants to get the trip started without frustration.

It's Augustus's first time flying and he's excited. He's also growing closer with Hazel. They watch the movie *300*. Augustus is impressed by the sacrifice of the soldiers in the story (sacrifice is a key component of his character). Hazel wonders about all the dead people in history, showing that her focus is generally more pessimistic than Augustus.

He tells her he loves her, but Hazel is unable to respond.

CHAPTER 11: Hazel, her mom, and Augustus arrive in Amsterdam. As the driver brings them closer to the town center the buildings get older. Hazel, with death never far from her thoughts, thinks that all the buildings around them were built by the dead. Their driver describes Amsterdam as a city of freedom.

They are staying at the Hotel Filosoof – a theme hotel in which each room is a tribute to a famous philosopher. Hazel's mom wants to go out and explore the city, but Hazel is tired, so they all stay in. This reminds us of the theme of sacrifice, even when it is small sacrifices like not sightseeing.

Hazel awakes later and gets ready for dinner with Augustus. They are going to dress up and go to a nice restaurant without Hazel's mom. It's a nearly perfect romantic dinner, with champagne and everything paid for by Peter Van Houten. This apparent generosity is setting up a major *anticlimax* when Peter Van Houten is finally introduced.

Augustus talks about sacrifice and death at the dinner. His ideas are sometimes at odds with Hazel, who thinks that a life matters even if there isn't a noble sacrifice involved. This minor conflict is soon smoothed over, and both of them are excited about meeting Van Houten the next day.

Hazel asks about Augustus's deceased ex-girlfriend, Caroline Mathers, and he tells the whole story. They met at the hospital when he was there. She was the only one using the swing on the hospital playground and he sought her out. She had brain cancer and it made her increasingly mean as her brain grew more and more affected. She would say mean things about everyone, including Augustus, making her death even more painful. Hazel is shocked by all this, and tells him she never wants to make him suffer like that. This connects to her self-image of being a grenade. But Augustus isn't concerned. He says, "It would be a privilege to have my heart broken by you."

CHAPTER 12: Hazel is nervous about meeting Van Houten. Not only is she meeting her favorite author, but she will finally get answers to her questions about *An Imperial Affliction*. Hazel wants the meeting to be perfect. She dresses like Anna, the main character in *AIA*. Her mom goes to sightsee while Hazel and Augustus go to their meeting.

They arrive at Peter Van Houten's house. From within they hear loud bass from a stereo. Hazel wonders if Van Houten has a teenage son. They knock on the door and are finally admitted. Peter Van Houten is not at all what they expect. He is a cranky old man who didn't actually expect them to come to Amsterdam. Most of the invitation (and the money spent on their dinner the night before) was coordinated by Van Houten's assistant Lidewij. She is polite and apologetic about Van Houten, who grows increasingly rude as he gets drunker.

Rather than answer Hazel's questions about *AIA*, Van Houten talks about Swedish hip hop and ancient philosophers. When he does finally address his novel, he gives flippant answers and tries to make Hazel see that the characters weren't real and therefore don't have a future after the events of the novel. His rudeness becomes too much for Lidewij. She angrily resigns her position as Van Houten's assistant.

Hazel feels cheated by the whole experience. Augustus finally pulls her out of the house. She regrets using Augustus's wish on Van Houten, but Augustus corrects her – the wish was used on *them*, not the rude author.

Lidewij comes out of the house and takes Hazel and Augustus to the Anne Frank house. On the way, she explains that she worked for Van Houten because his book "shaped real lives," but now she just views the man as a monster. Van Houten's income comes primarily from inventions made by his ancestors, she says.

There is no elevator to take them up in the Anne Frank house. Hazel insists that it's okay and climbs the stairs. It's a lot of work for her, but she feels she owes it to Anne Frank, who did nothing wrong but still suffered and died horribly.

At the top of the house a video of Anne Frank's father is playing, explaining how parents don't really know their children. This connects to Hazel's own disconnected moments (and arguments later in the book) from her parents. As the video plays, she and Augustus kiss. Hazel is briefly concerned it might be offensive to kiss in the Anne Frank house, but quickly decides that Anne Frank would approve. The other tourists there also approve, applauding the young couple.

After the museum, Hazel suggests they go to Augustus's hotel room. He hesitates on the way and she views it as unwillingness to be intimate with her. It's actually his own nervousness about his amputated leg. She tells him it's not an issue, and we can see that it isn't, that these two are in love, regardless of what the world or their bodies have to say about it.

They have sex and it is awkward and quiet, bringing them closer together than ever.

CHAPTER 13: Hazel recounts to her mother the visit to Van Houten, giving it a humorous tone. She tells the reader about Maslow's Hierarchy of Needs, a psychological idea put forth by Abraham Maslow that a person can't focus on higher needs (like self-actualization) until basic needs are met. Hazel interprets this to mean that people such as she and Augustus (who don't have their basic survival assured because of their cancer) can't go on to fulfill higher needs. Hazel thinks this is ridiculous.

Augustus has given signs, but it wasn't until now that Hazel realizes he is not well. He didn't tell her but before the trip he felt a pain in his hip. He had a PET scan and his cancer was throughout his body. The chemo he started wasn't working and he stopped it just before the trip, leading to the fight with his parents that Hazel overheard.

Hazel views Augustus's drive for meaning as a refutation of Maslow's Hierarchy. He was determined to go to Amsterdam with Hazel even though his survival is in jeopardy. Now that *he* is the "grenade," the situation reversed, she knows that it doesn't matter. She loves him and that is all that matters.

CHAPTER 14: They fly back to Indiana. Augustus remembers a science teacher he once had who took the magic out of everything he discussed, making the world a cold reality. Van Houten was like that – his words may have been true, but he said them in an unnecessarily cruel way.

They drink champagne on the plane until Augustus experiences chest pains. He takes some pain medication and sleeps.

Hazel's dad meets them at the airport. He read *An Imperial Affliction* while they were gone and Hazel enjoys hanging out with him again. They discuss their different attitudes, similar to Hazel and Augustus, and Hazel's dad is generally more optimistic than she is. Rather than meaningless, he says that "the universe wants to be noticed."

Augustus is on new cancer drugs. Isaac comes over to hang out with them. He still hasn't had any word from Monica, his ex-girlfriend. Augustus thinks this is plain wrong. They go to her house and throw eggs at her car. It's very cathartic for both Augustus and Isaac. It's not about Monica, says Augustus, and he doesn't care if she's home or not to witness the vandalism. Monica's mom even comes out of the house at one point, and Augustus shames her into going away.

Hazel takes a photo of Isaac and Augustus, and says it's the last photo she ever took of her boyfriend, foreshadowing his impending death and adding to the suspense.

CHAPTER 15: A meal takes place at Augustus's house with Hazel's family attending. Augustus has more chest pains soon after. He must go to the hospital. Hazel tries to see him there but Augustus's mom wants to limit visitors to family, for a while anyway.

Augustus is in a wheelchair after that. Hazel takes him to "Funky Bones," the outdoor art exhibit they visited early in the book. They have champagne again. Augustus senses his approaching death and there are other hints that he'll be gone soon.

CHAPTER 16: Augustus is tired, thin, and sick. He wants to write a sequel to *AIA* for Hazel to tie up the loose ends, but he's too tired to do it. He decides to tell her his version of what happens to the characters as soon as he figures it all out.

He's getting nutrition through a G-tube, a tube directly to his digestive system (so he doesn't have to chew food and risk vomiting it up). He's confined to a wheelchair, but he can still push himself around. They are trying to make things as "normal" as possible for them, and they have a nostalgia for the way things used to be.

CHAPTER 17: Augustus continues to deteriorate. He is very drugged up and pisses his bed. Hazel makes a hurtful remark about what he's become, and they try to carry on.

CHAPTER 18: Hazel gets a call from Augustus at 2:35 in the morning (at first she thinks it might be his parents calling to say he has died). He's at a gas station and he needs Hazel's help. She's confused and wants to call 911, but he just wants her to come, so she does. She finds him parked in his car and covered in his own vomit. She calls 911 as he pukes again. His G-tube is giving him trouble. All he wanted to do was go to the gas station and buy a pack of cigarettes, to show himself he was still capable of that, but apparently he isn't.

Far from the cliché of the "noble" cancer patient who stoically faces his disease, Augustus just wants to die. He realizes there is no epic battle to be fought, that there are no "bad guys." Even his cancer only wants to live.

He asks Hazel for a poem. The only one she can think of is a short one by William Carlos Williams. She adds to it, and Augustus says, "And you say you don't write poetry."

John Green doesn't sugarcoat the process of Augustus's illness. It is getting increasingly ugly, but the fact that Hazel's love can persist shows that it's genuine.

CHAPTER 19: Augustus is permanently moved upstairs in his house. He realizes the burden he is on other people.

Hazel arrives one day to find relatives there she's never met before, including some of Augustus's bratty nephews. Augustus wakes up and goes with Hazel and the others outside. Everybody is being *too* nice to Augustus, so Hazel gives him some of her usual sarcasm, the only one really treating him *normal*. It mirrors the little girl Hazel met at the mall who treated Hazel normally. Augustus's dad kisses Hazel on the cheek and thanks her.

She gives further hints Augustus will die soon.

CHAPTER 20: Augustus asks Hazel to write him a eulogy and meet him in "the literal heart of Jesus," the church location of the cancer support group. Her parents are angry Hazel is often away from home, visiting Augustus, and she bitterly talks back to them, saying that she'll be home all the time once Augustus is dead. She is rude, but her parents also step back and give her some freedom.

She arrives at the church and finds Augustus and Isaac there for a *prefuneral*. Augustus wants to attend his own funeral, and this seems like the easiest way to do it. Isaac gives a snarky speech about Augustus, but it reveals how good of friends they are. Hazel then gives her speech, referencing Peter Van Houten's claim that "some infinities are bigger than other infinities." She acknowledges the depth of her love for Augustus, and we as readers can begin to understand what she'll experience when her boyfriend dies (in the next chapter).

CHAPTER 21: Augustus dies eight days after his "prefuneral." She informs Isaac about Augustus's death, but then realizes she doesn't want to talk to anyone else about it (except Augustus). Plus, losing Augustus is like losing part of the memories that they shared together, somehow making those experiences less real.

The pain of his absence feels unbearable to Hazel. She looks at his online profile. Countless people have left messages of condolence. She doesn't know who they are and she's bitter that they're coming out of the woodwork now. Where were they when Augustus was sick and dying?

Augustus's real funeral is scheduled for five days after his death. If the people leaving messages are representative of those who'll be at the funeral, she thinks she'll vomit. She posts her own honest reflection on Augustus's death and it's quickly lost in the other messages.

Hazel's parents want to help her and ask what they can do. She and her family have forgiven each other for the things they said and did, and she embraces them for comfort.

CHAPTER 22: The funeral for Augustus takes place. Hazel gets and gives hugs, but she largely feels like she's alone in mourning. The minister describes how Augustus will be "whole" again in heaven, and from behind her Hazel hears the voice of Peter Van Houten say, "What a load of horse crap, eh, kid?" She is shocked by the author's sudden appearance.

The service continues and various people speak about Augustus, including Isaac. When Hazel's turn comes, rather than giving a humorous and sarcastic eulogy, she gives a standard talk filled with sentimentality. She thinks, "Funerals, I had decided, are for the living."

Hazel just wants to go home and get away from all the people. She is sad, but must go to the burial. She makes it through, and Peter Van Houten explains to her that he corresponded through letters with Augustus before his death. When the boy finally died, Van Houten bought a first-class ticket to be at the funeral. Van Houten does his best to give Hazel some kind of consolation, even offering an ending to *An Imperial Affliction*, but she is in no mood to deal with the author.

At home, Hazel's dad offers a few words of consolation that mean a great deal to her. We can see that she'll be sad for a long time, but that she'll recover.

CHAPTER 23: Hazel visits Isaac, and while they're playing his audio game they make an attempt at humor, until Isaac says, "I dislike living in a world without Augustus Waters." Then Isaac mentions the "sequel" to *AIA* that Augustus was working on before his death. He'd mentioned it to Isaac a month earlier. Hazel had never heard about this (beyond vague conjecture), and she's suddenly determined to have this final message from Augustus.

She leaves to go to Augustus's parents, but is startled to find Peter Van Houten in the minivan she's driving. He's been drinking and he frightens her until she realizes he's harmless, and recognizes that he once lost a child to illness. Hazel listens and learns that Van Houten had a daughter who he lost to leukemia when she was eight. Hazel is able to finally sympathize with the man, and they reach a kind of peace. She encourages him to sober up and write again, but as she leaves she sees him sipping his alcohol.

At Augustus's house his parents are kind. They allow Hazel to look through his things for any writing he might have left behind. She can't find anything, however. His parents discourage any further search. Augustus was very sick and tired in his final month. He couldn't have written anything, they tell her, but she is not so easily dissuaded in her search.

CHAPTER 24: Hazel receives a phone call from Augustus's parents: They've found a notebook near his hospital bed, but there is no writing, only signs that some pages have been ripped out. Hazel wonders where the pages might be. Perhaps Augustus left them at the church when they did his "prefuneral." She decides to go to the cancer support group (held in the same church) to check.

She goes through the usual routine of the support group, but she has genuine sadness that can't be overcome in one evening. She also can't find any of the pages there.

She gets home and has a small argument with her mother about eating dinner. Her mom refuses to let her fall to pieces over Augustus's death. Hazel cruelly says that she will die and her mom won't be a mother anymore. This is a fear she overheard her mother say earlier in the book. Her mom is shocked that Hazel overheard it, but says that she'll always be Hazel's mother, because she'll always love her.

Her mom also reveals that she's been studying to get a master's degree in social work. This is a pleasant surprise for Hazel, and she's beginning to feel less like a grenade.

CHAPTER 25: Talking with Kaitlyn, Hazel realizes that Augustus may have mailed the missing notebook pages to someone: Peter Van Houten. She immediately emails Lidewij in Amsterdam, and the woman promises to search Van Houten's house. If the letter was sent to the author, Lidewij will make him read it. Lidewij was unaware of Augustus's death and it saddens her.

Hazel's mom informs her that it's Bastille Day, a major French holiday, but not particularly important in America. Still, they use it as an excuse to go to nearby Holliday Park together as a family. The weather is nice, and they also visit Augustus's grave.

An email eventually comes from Lidewij, who has visited Van Houten. There is an attachment with the email, and it *is* the pages Augustus sent Van Houten, in which he asked the author to write a eulogy for Hazel. He explains to Van Houten why Hazel is different, and it no doubt flatters Hazel and serves as a fitting reminder of why she loves Augustus.

Augustus thought that Hazel would die before him. He concludes his letter saying, "You don't get to choose if you get hurt in this world... but you do have some say in who hurts you. I like my choices."\Hazel confirms that she likes her choices as well. She's come to realize it's a privilege to allow someone into your heart, knowing full well it will ultimately hurt you.

CRITICAL QUESTIONS & ESSAY TOPICS

These critical questions may be answered in a variety of ways based on your reading of the text. I have provided suggestions in the answers below, and I encourage you to consider alternative answers as you explore these topics.

1. How does John Green avoid the clichés of the "cancer kid genre"?

Green self-consciously refers to the "cancer kid genre," stories about cancer patients and how they bravely face their cancer with humor, learning about themselves and the beauty of life through a series of epiphanies. Hazel is very familiar with these stories. Because of her cynical perspective, she tears these clichés apart any time she sees them appearing. She has seen enough of the realities of cancer to know that it's sometimes painful, pointless, and messy.

Hazel is also disappointed and angered by her meeting with Peter Van Houten, the unexpected return of Augustus's cancer, and her conflict with her parents. Her cancer lifestyle often brings out her darker side, and it is far from her ideal personality.

2. What role does *An Imperial Affliction* play in the novel?

An Imperial Affliction, Hazel's favorite novel, gives us insight into her own concerns and identity. She sees in the character of Anna someone who she can relate to, someone who understands what living (and dying) with cancer is like. Her non-ill friends and family may have compassion for her, but they don't share the same experiences as her. *An Imperial Affliction* is a book she can always look to for *empathy*. And although we only get small excerpts of this book-within-the-book, Hazel and Augustus both say it is well written. Their obsession can also be attributed to the mysterious elements in the book that go unanswered, even after meeting Van Houten.

3. Is Peter Van Houten a sympathetic character?

Whether Van Houten is sympathetic is, of course, up to the reader. Initially, however, when we see him in Amsterdam there is little to like about him. He is rude, drunk, and annoying. Later, we learn that his daughter died young, and he also shows up at Augustus's funeral. We see that he is struggling with alcoholism, and this makes him slightly more sympathetic, if not likable.

It's worth noting that Hazel is able to maintain her admiration for *An Imperial Affliction* and the mind that conceived it, and keep that admiration separate from the current version of Van Houten. She does seem more willing to sympathize with Van Houten by the end of the novel.

4. Describe Hazel's relationship with her parents through the novel.

For the majority of the novel, Hazel and her parents get along well. She has cheeky responses and is often more cynical than they are, but the family members love each other. It is only with the stress that accompanies Augustus's illness that Hazel and her parents have serious problems. They want to spend time with her and have the same relationship they've always had. She has other plans because her time with Augustus is limited.

Hazel's parents eventually give her more freedom, and she realizes that she doesn't want to distance them from her.

5. How would the story be different if Hazel and Augustus were adults?

Much of the conflict faced by Augustus and Hazel is unique to teenagers. They are largely dependent on their parents. They have limited experience with relationships, sex, and death. They can face some of these challenges together. However, Hazel must face Augustus's death (obviously) without him. All of these conditions brought about by their young age make for greater struggle and more opportunities for growth in the characters. Some situations would be similar if Hazel and Augustus were adults, but some of the situations (like their first sexual experience) are unique to the *young adult* genre.

6. Why does Augustus address his final letter to Peter Van Houten and not Hazel?

Having already spent a great deal of time with Hazel and said everything he is able to say, it's possible that Augustus wrote Van Houten to help voice the things he *wasn't* able to say. Perhaps Augustus hopes to fulfill the promise of their trip to Amsterdam. They had such high hopes about Van Houten, and Augustus may feel that the trip disappointed Hazel.

It's also possible that Augustus knew that Hazel would eventually see the final letter he sent, or at least hoped she would.

7. How does the relationship between Isaac and Monica compare to Hazel and Augustus?

Isaac and Monica's relationship is depicted as youthful love. The couple constantly exchanges messages with the word "always," yet when their love faces the challenge of Isaac's blindness, we see just how flimsy their love really is. It's tempting to blame Monica completely for abandoning the relationship, but Isaac eventually turns his back on it as well, throwing eggs at Monica's car to resolve his rage.

Hazel and Augustus, on the other hand, show more maturity in their relationship, persevering through Augustus's illness, aware that it will not always be pretty.

8. How are death and the afterlife viewed by characters in the novel?

A wide variety of views are presented by different characters in the book. Some, like Van Houten, have strong existential perspectives. They think that this life is all we have, and when we die there is nothing more. Others, like Augustus's parents, show perspective closer to orthodox Christianity.

Hazel is closer to the existential side of things for most of the book (Van Houten's novel is her favorite book, after all). Yet she does show she is open to other perspectives, especially when her dad relates his story about how the universe "wants to be noticed." Augustus also seems to believe that there is something more, and that our lives have meaning. John Green doesn't try to force any one viewpoint on the reader, but he does offer the possibility to people like Hazel that existence has true significance.

CONCLUSION

The Fault in Our Stars has proven to be a universal story, affecting countless readers with its strong characters, dark humor, and penetrating questions. I hope this guide has helped you navigate the book, and deepened your understanding of all that occurs in its pages.

Made in the USA
Columbia, SC
05 May 2021

37403082R00026